WE BOTH READ

Parent's Introduction

We Both Read is the first series of books designed to invite parents and children to share the reading of a story by taking turns reading aloud. This "shared reading" innovation, which was developed with reading education specialists, invites parents to read the more complex text and storyline on the left-hand pages. Then, children can be encouraged to read the right-hand pages, which feature less complex text and storyline, specifically written for the beginning reader.

Reading aloud is one of the most important activities parents can share with their child to assist them in their reading development. However, *We Both Read* goes beyond reading *to* a child and allows parents to share the reading *with* a child. *We Both Read* is so powerful and effective because it combines two key elements in learning: "modeling" (the parent reads) and "doing" (the child reads). The result is not only faster reading development for the child, but a much more enjoyable and enriching experience for both!

You may find it helpful to read the entire book aloud yourself the first time, then invite your child to participate in the second reading. In some books, a few more difficult words will first be introduced in the parent's text, distinguished with **bold lettering**. Pointing out, and even discussing, these words will help familiarize your child with them and help to build your child's vocabulary. Also, note that a "talking parent" icon ⑥ precedes the parent's text and a "talking child" icon ⑥ precedes the child's text.

We encourage you to share and interact with your child as you read the book together. If your child is having difficulty, you might want to mention a few things to help them. "Sounding out" is good, but it will not work with all words. Children can pick up clues about the words they are reading from the story, the context of the sentence, or even the pictures. Some stories have rhyming patterns that might help. It might also help them to touch the words with their finger as they read, to better connect the voice sound and the printed word.

Sharing the *We Both Read* books together will engage you and your child in an interactive adventure in reading! It is a fun and easy way to encourage and help your child to read—and a wonderful way to start them off on a lif

We Both Read: President Theodore Roosevelt

———————————————————————

Text Copyright © 2006 by Sindy McKay
Illustrations Copyright © 2006 by John Gampert
Use of photography provided by the Theodore Roosevelt Collection,
Harvard College Library (pp. 1, 3, 5, 8, 11, 15, 18, 20, 22, 23, 26, 27, 35, 36, & 38)
and Sagamore Hill National Historic Site (pp. 9, 13, 24, 31, & 32).
All rights reserved

We Both Read® is a trademark of Treasure Bay, Inc.

Published by Treasure Bay, Inc.
40 Sir Francis Drake Boulevard
San Anselmo, CA 94960 USA

PRINTED IN SINGAPORE

Library of Congress Catalog Card Number: 2005905161

Hardcover ISBN: 1-891327-67-4 *3296 9890 4/06*
Paperback ISBN: 1-891327-68-2

We Both Read® Books
Patent No. 5,957,693

Visit us online at:
www.webothread.com

President Theodore Roosevelt

By Sindy McKay

Illustrated by John Gampert

TREASURE BAY

 Have you ever seen a picture of the Grand Canyon, watched a football game, or owned a teddy bear? If so, you already know a little something about the 26th President of the United States, **Theodore Roosevelt**.

Theodore Roosevelt was a very popular President, who cared about all people, rich and poor. He also cared about nature and saving it for the future.

Theodore "Teddy" Roosevelt was born in New York on Oct. 27, 1858. As a child, he was often ill. He suffered terribly from asthma, sometimes struggling just to breathe.

Teddy's father told him, "You have the mind, but you don't have the body. You must make your body." So Teddy began to exercise and spend lots of time outdoors in nature to build up his strength.

   Young Teddy loved to read and to draw pictures of nature.

He also loved to hike. He would gather things like leaves, rocks, and old bird nests along the way.

Theodore Roosevelt in a group picture for the Harvard Advocate,
a literary magazine. Theodore was the editor of the magazine.

Theodore's strong interest in nature led him to Harvard
University in Massachusetts where he studied to be a naturalist.
Naturalists are scientists who **study** plants and animals.

Theodore loved learning about nature. He also wanted to help people, so he began to **study** law as well.

At age 22, Theodore Roosevelt married his first wife, Alice Lee, and they lived happily together in New York City. A year later, Teddy became the youngest person ever elected to the New York State Assembly.

Theodore felt that everyone who worked in **government** should be working for the good of the people.

President Roosevelt on a New England speaking tour, Aug. 1902

Beliefs / philosophy

He felt that all **government** workers should do their job well. He also felt that people should know how the government was spending their tax money.

Alice Roosevelt, the first of President Roosevelt's six children

 Things were going well for the Roosevelts and Theodore was delighted when, in February of 1884, his wife gave birth to a baby girl. They named her Alice, after her mother.

Then tragedy struck. Shortly after baby Alice was born, Theodore's wife and his mother both died on the same day.

Theodore lost two of the people he loved most in the world. His heart was broken.

   Theodore was so devastated by his loss that he left New York and traveled to the Dakota Territory where he purchased two small cattle ranches. For the next two years, he worked as a cowboy, spending all day in the saddle.

Theodore's love of nature helped him mend his broken heart. He believed that spending time outdoors was the best way to heal the body and the mind.

Edith Roosevelt, President Roosevelt's second wife.
Theodore and Edith were married in 1886.

In late 1885, young Roosevelt returned to New York where he soon married his second wife, an old childhood sweetheart named **Edith** Carow. Together they had five children.

Theodore and **Edith** had four boys and one girl. They joined Theodore's first daughter Alice to become a happy family of six children.

Theodore Roosevelt and the Rough Riders atop San Juan Heights, after the July 1st battle.

Mr. Roosevelt joined the military during the Spanish-American War. He commanded his own group of soldiers, who were called the "Rough Riders." He became a war hero when he led his men in a charge up **San Juan Heights** in Cuba.

 Theodore Roosevelt was given the Medal of Honor in 2001 for his bravery at **San Juan Heights**. This was long after he had died. He is the only U.S. President to receive this honor.

After the war, Theodore Roosevelt was elected the Governor of New York State. He worked hard to improve the working conditions of New Yorkers, especially the women and children.

Two years later, Governor Roosevelt was asked to run for Vice President with William McKinley.

McKinley/Roosevelt Presidential Campaign. Ramapo Iron works, Hillburn, NY, Fall 1900.

Roosevelt didn't really want to run for Vice President. He said, "It is not an office in which I can *do* anything."

However, he did run. On March 4, 1901, he became Vice President of the United States.

Six months later, President McKinley was assassinated. He was shot by a crazed gunman while greeting people at the Pan-American Exposition in Buffalo, New York. Eight days after he was shot, McKinley died and Vice President Roosevelt became President Roosevelt.

President Theodore Roosevelt, The White House, 1903

Theodore Roosevelt became the youngest President in United States history. He was just 42 years old.

President Roosevelt did many good things for this country. During his first term in office, he helped make working conditions safer for people, like the coal miners, who did manual labor. He fought against big companies that did not pay their workers a fair wage.

President Roosevelt speaking at Northwestern University, Evanston, IL., April 2, 1903

 President Roosevelt wanted every person in America to have a "square deal." That means he wanted every worker to be treated fairly.

President Roosevelt with Russian and Japanese envoys aboard Mayflower, the Presidential yacht, Aug. 5, 1905

In 1904, President Roosevelt was elected to a second term. During his second term, he won the Nobel Peace Prize for helping to peacefully end the Russo-Japanese War. He is the only President to have received this prestigious award while still in office.

Theodore Roosevelt sits at his desk at Sagamore Hill, which was his home and where he often worked during the summer. Sagamore Hill, located in Oyster Bay, New York, is now a National Historic Site and is open to the public.

President Roosevelt felt that our food, water, and medicine should always be safe. He worked to pass a law to make sure it would be safe.

While he was President, the President's mansion officially became known as the White House.

Roosevelt's six children had lots of **energy** and they soon became known as "the White House Gang" because they loved to slide down the banisters and roller skate in the halls!

 The people who wrote for the newspapers called President Roosevelt "T. R." or "Teddy". They liked writing about him because he was so young and full of **energy**!

Cartoon of Theodore Roosevelt and a young bear by Clifford Berryman.
This cartoon appeared in the Washington Post, Nov. 16, 1902.

President Roosevelt still loved the outdoors and he often spent time hunting, fishing, and hiking.

One day a newspaper reported that the **popular** President had spared the life of a young bear cub while hunting. A shop-keeper asked permission to display a toy bear in his window with a sign that read "Teddy's bear."

Soon there were stores all over the country selling teddy bears. They became very **popular**. They are still very popular today.

Football was one of T.R.'s favorite sports. But back in 1905, football was so brutal that it was almost banned.

President Roosevelt urged the major colleges to create a new set of rules for the game. His interest in making college sports less dangerous for the **athletes** led to the formation of the National College Athletic Association—the NCAA—in 1906.

 Football is still a very popular sport today. Thanks to President Roosevelt, it is much safer to play.

Theodore Roosevelt embraced new technology in 1910 during his trip to St. Louis, when he accompanied pilot Arch Hoxsey into the air on a bi-plane.

It's hard to imagine it now, but Roosevelt was the very first President to fly in an airplane!

In fact, T.R. accomplished many Presidential "firsts". He was the first to travel outside of the U.S. while still in office, traveling to Panama to check on the progress of the Panama Canal.

Theodore Roosevelt enjoyed traveling throughout the United States.

Roosevelt was the first President to dive in a submarine. He was also the first to have a telephone in his home and the first to own his own car.

Grand Canyon National Park, Arizona

President Roosevelt is also considered to be the first "conservation" President. He wanted to preserve the **natural** beauty of our country for future generations.

In 1908, he made a Presidential Proclamation to set aside 800,000 acres in Arizona as the Grand Canyon National Monument.

Roosevelt felt that the Grand Canyon was the one great sight that every American should see. He wanted to be sure it would always be left in its **natural** state.

President Roosevelt in Yosemite with John Muir, May 1903

○ During his two terms in office, Roosevelt helped to create 51 wildlife reserves, 16 national monuments, and 5 new national parks. He also set aside 235 million acres of land as national forests.

 President Roosevelt once said, "We are not building this country of ours for a day. It is to last through the ages."

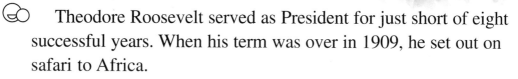

Theodore Roosevelt served as President for just short of eight successful years. When his term was over in 1909, he set out on safari to Africa.

In 1914, Theodore and his son Kermit joined an expedition to explore several uncharted areas of the Brazilian **jungle** to chart the course of a river called the **River of Doubt**.

Theodore Roosevelt starting down the River of Doubt, Feb. 28, 1914

T.R. was badly hurt when he cut his leg on a sharp rock. He became very ill and almost didn't make it out of the **jungle** alive. In his honor, the **River of Doubt** is now called the Rio Roosevelt.

Mount Rushmore National Memorial, South Dakota

In 1919, Theodore Roosevelt died in his sleep at the age of 60. He is considered one of our great Presidents and is one of the four faces carved on South Dakota's Mount Rushmore, along with George Washington, Thomas Jefferson, and Abraham Lincoln.

Roosevelt once said, "It is hard to fail, but it is worse never to have tried to **succeed**."

Theodore Roosevelt always tried hard to **succeed**. By trying hard, he **succeeded** in making our country a better place for all of us.

If you liked
President Theodore Roosevelt, here are two other
We Both Read® Books you are sure to enjoy!

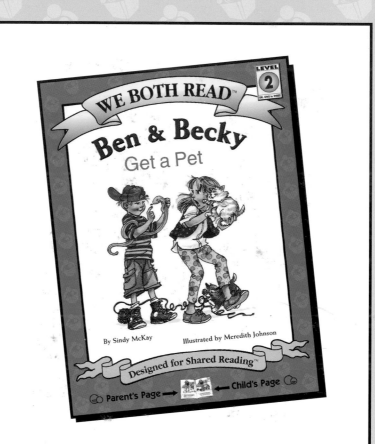

Ben and Becky finally convince their parents to let them have a pet. Becky wants to get a kitten, but Ben wants to get a snake. They go with their father to pick out a pet and cause hilarious excitement when they accidentally let the pet store's snake loose in the mall!